FUCK OFF SERIES

Amusing Swear Words To Color

For Stress Releasing

By
Queenie McJody

Happy Coloring!

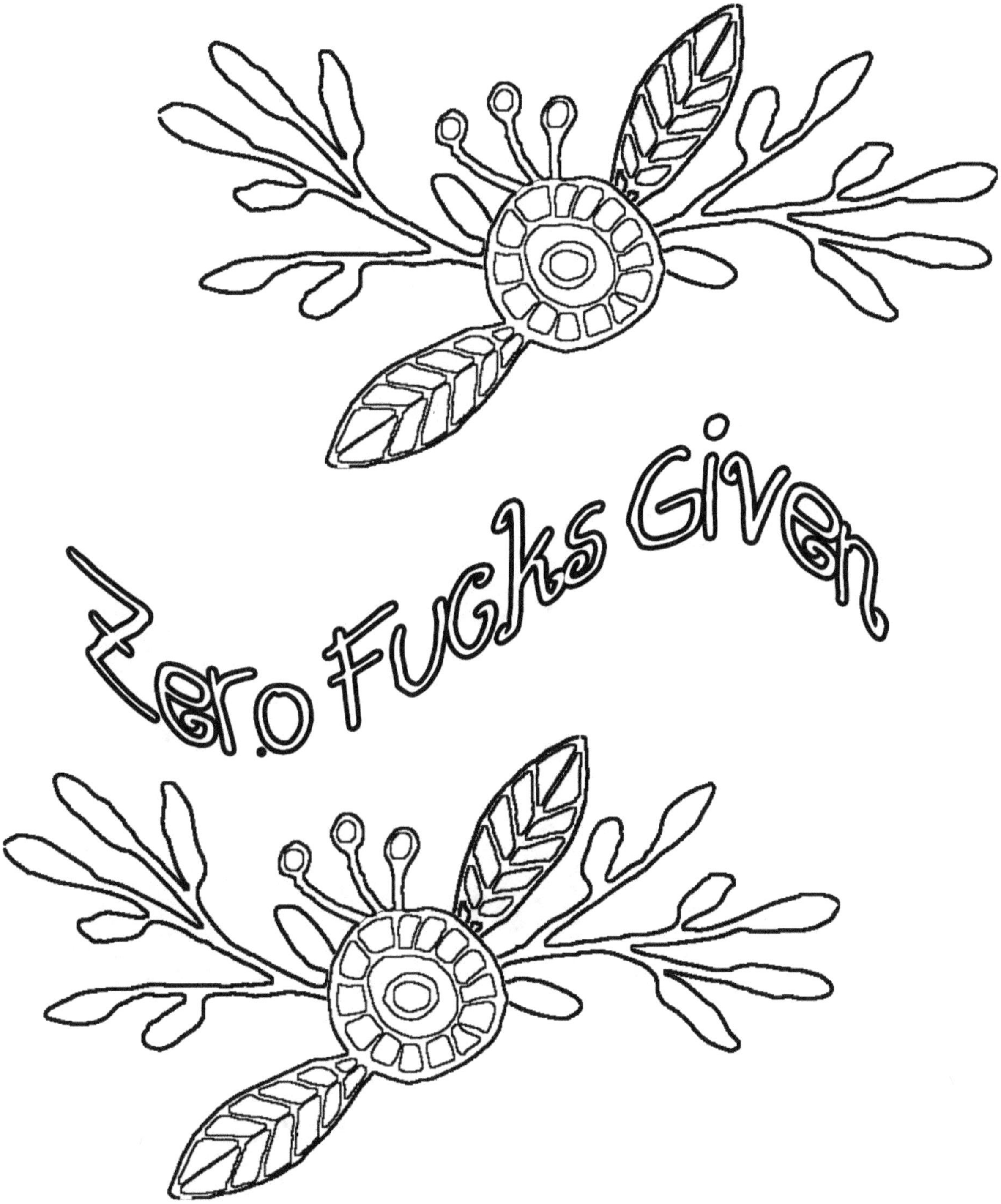
Zero Fucks Given

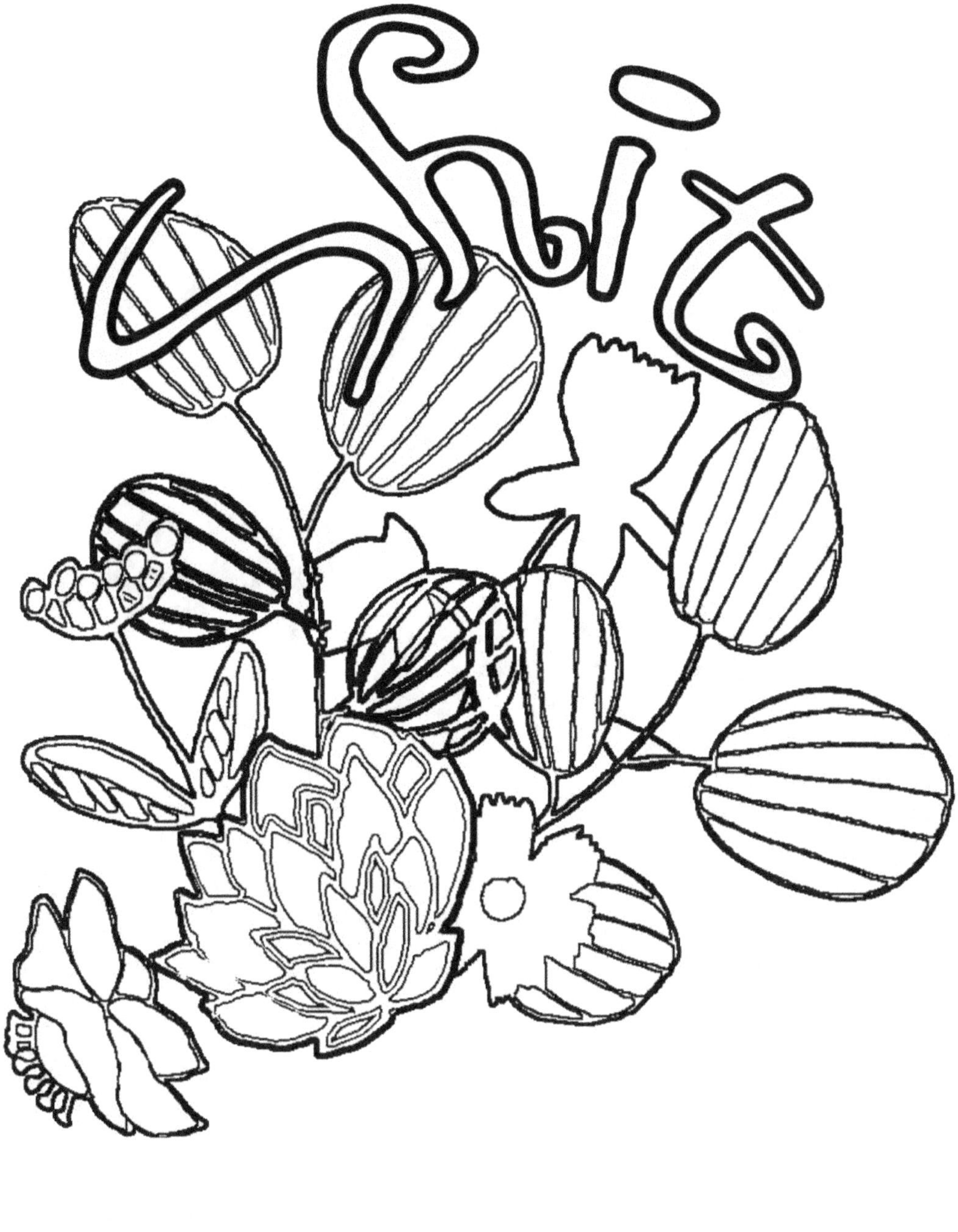
Shit

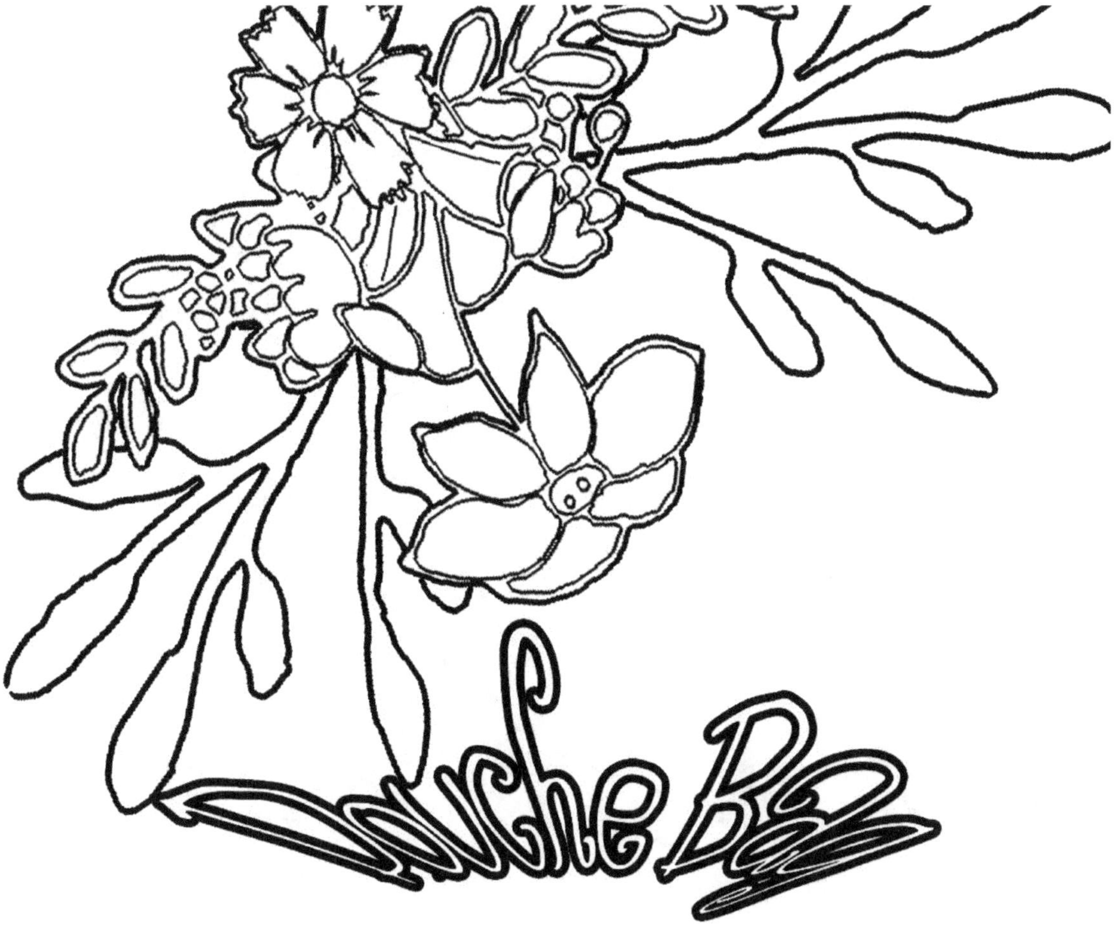
Douche Bag

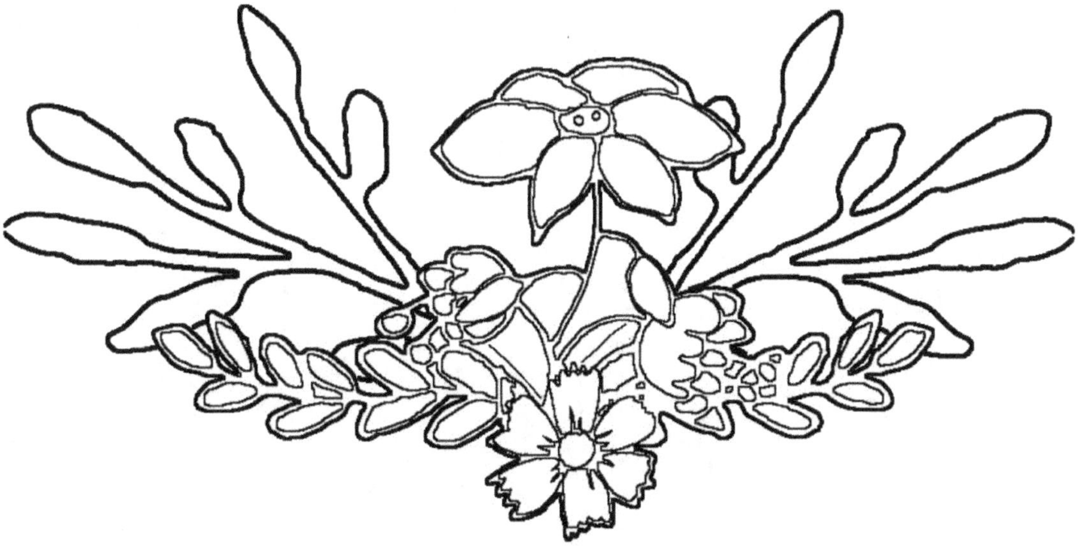

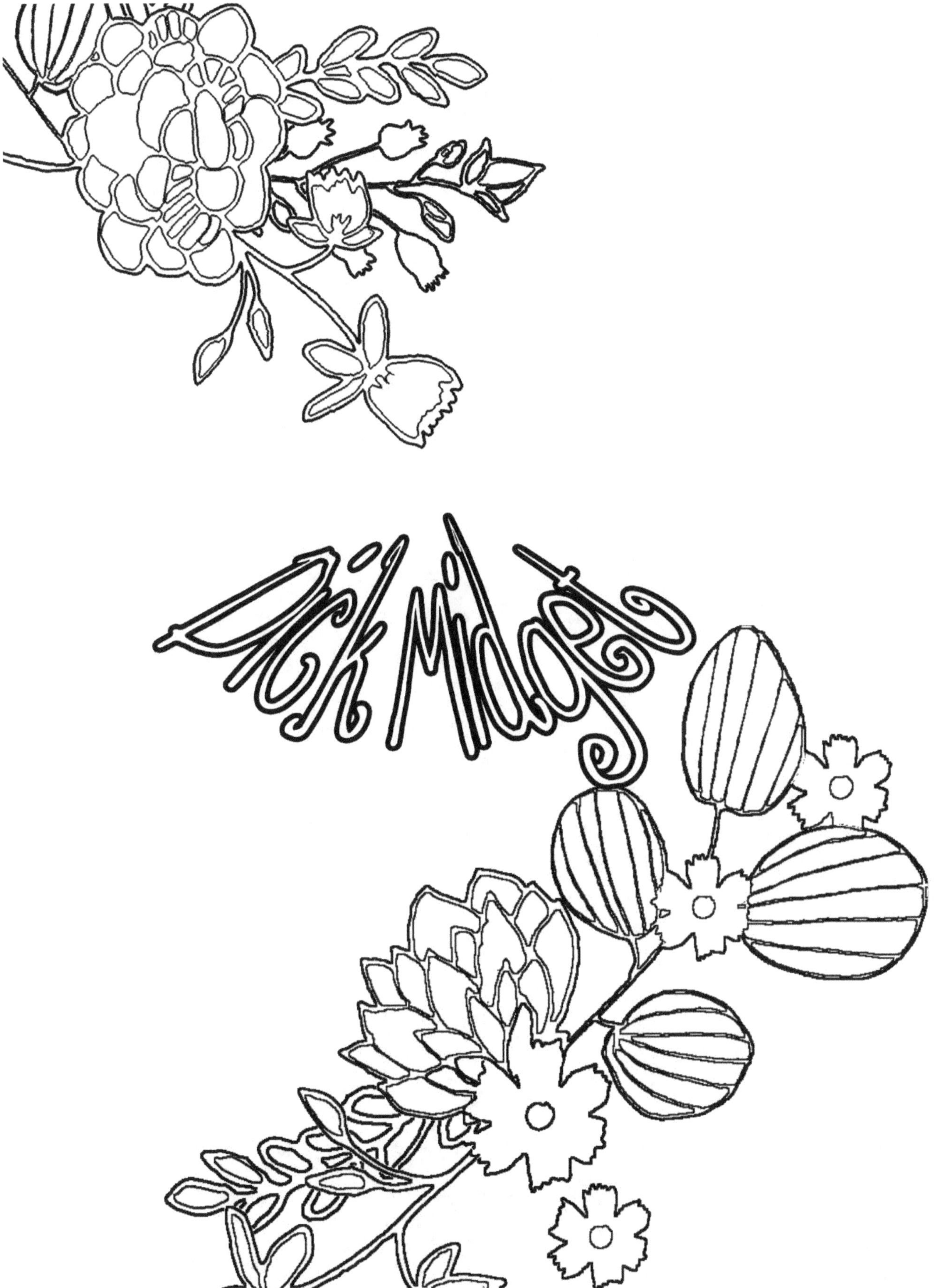
Dick Midget

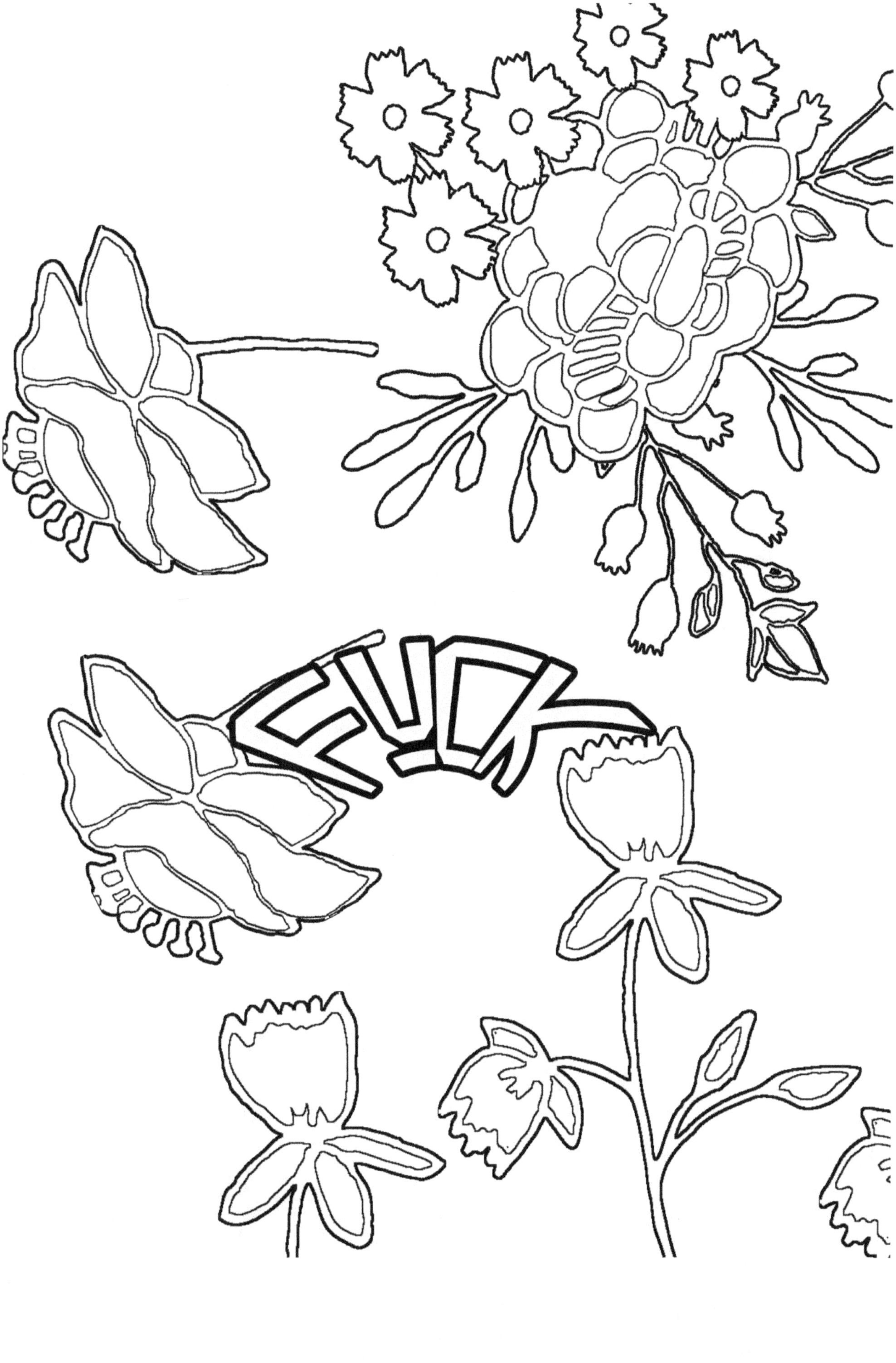
FUCK

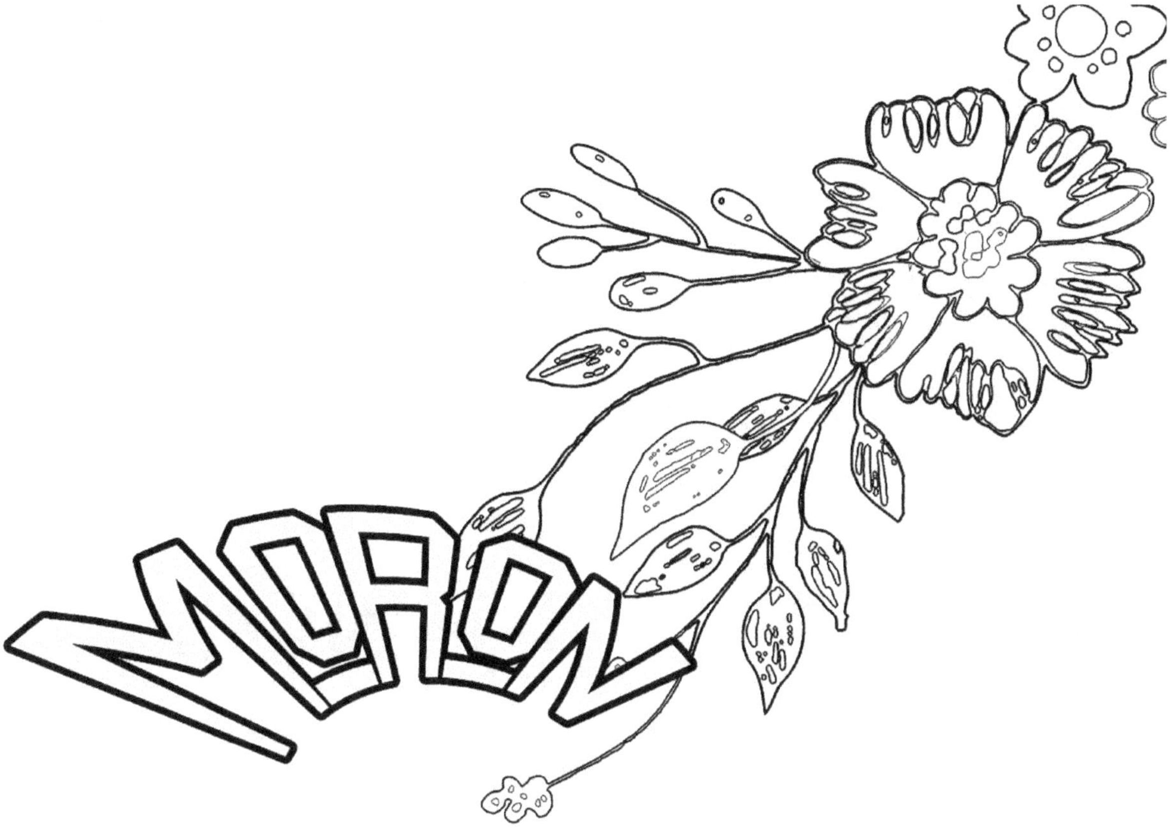
MORON

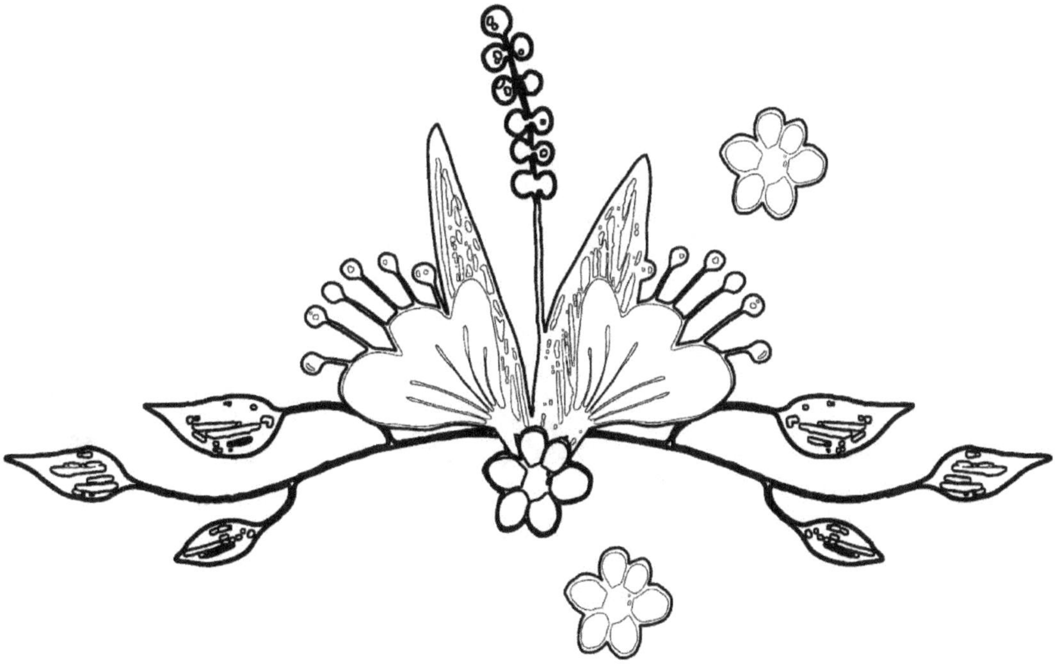

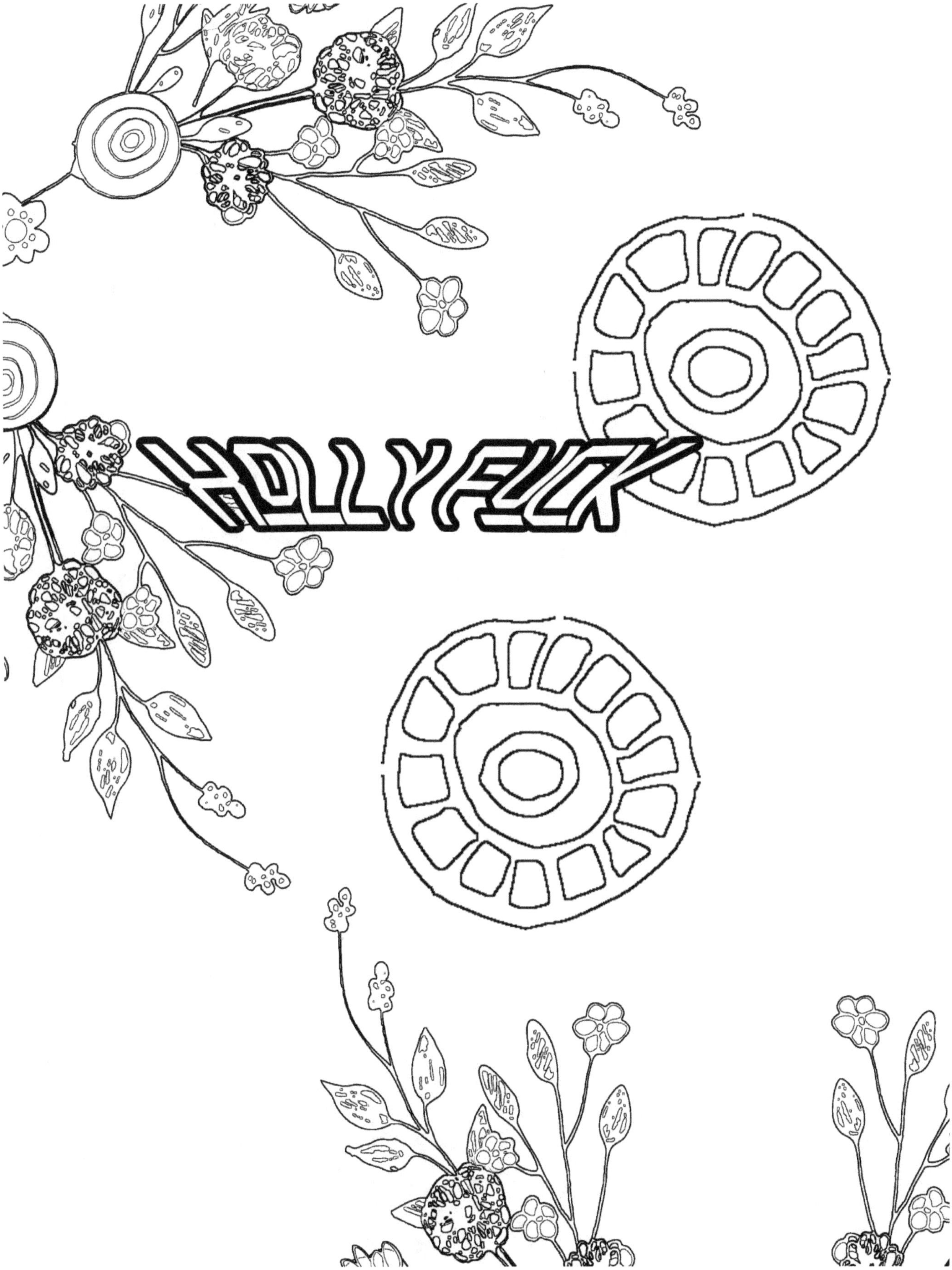
HOLLY FUCK

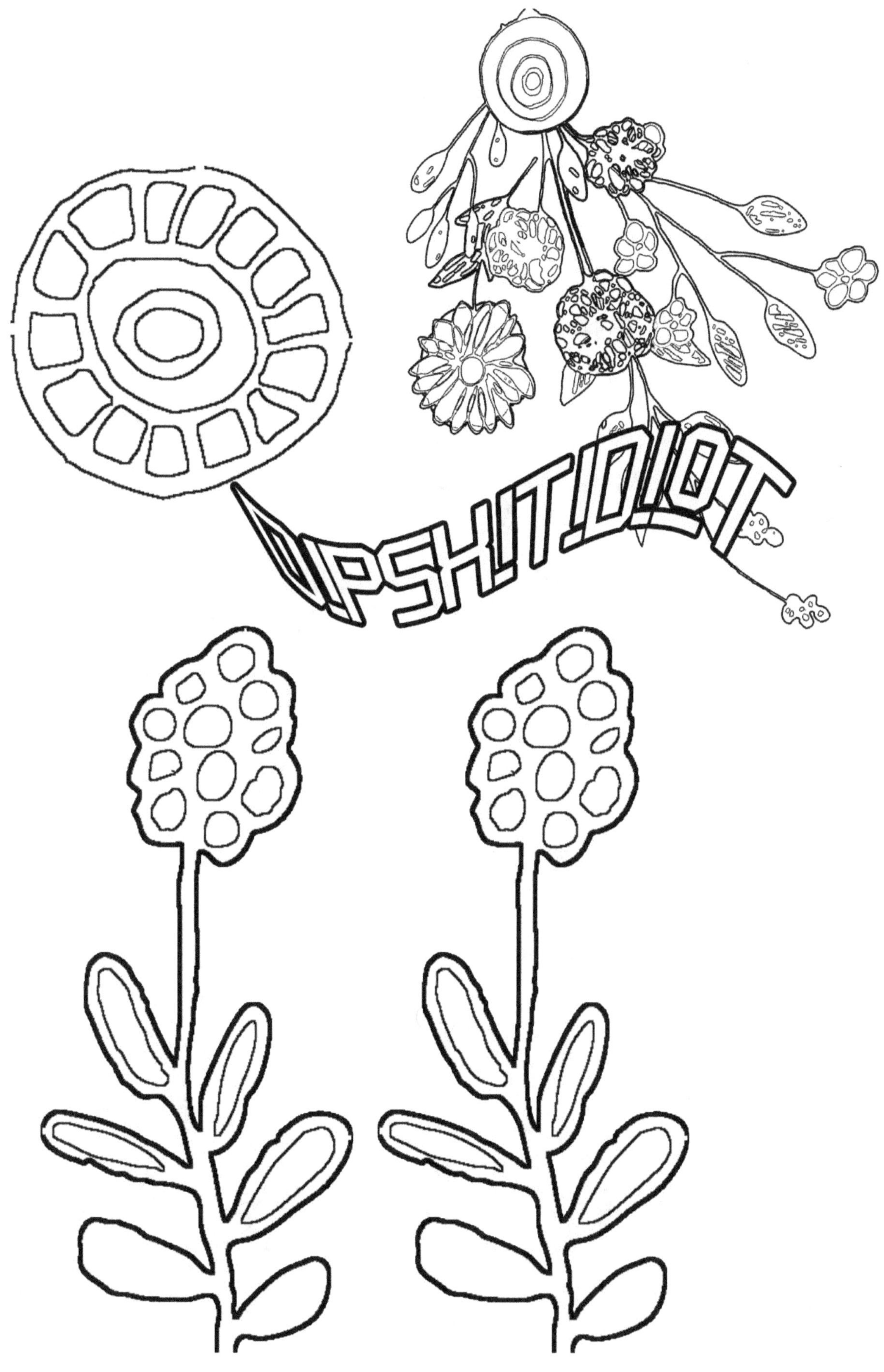
DIPSHIT IDIOT

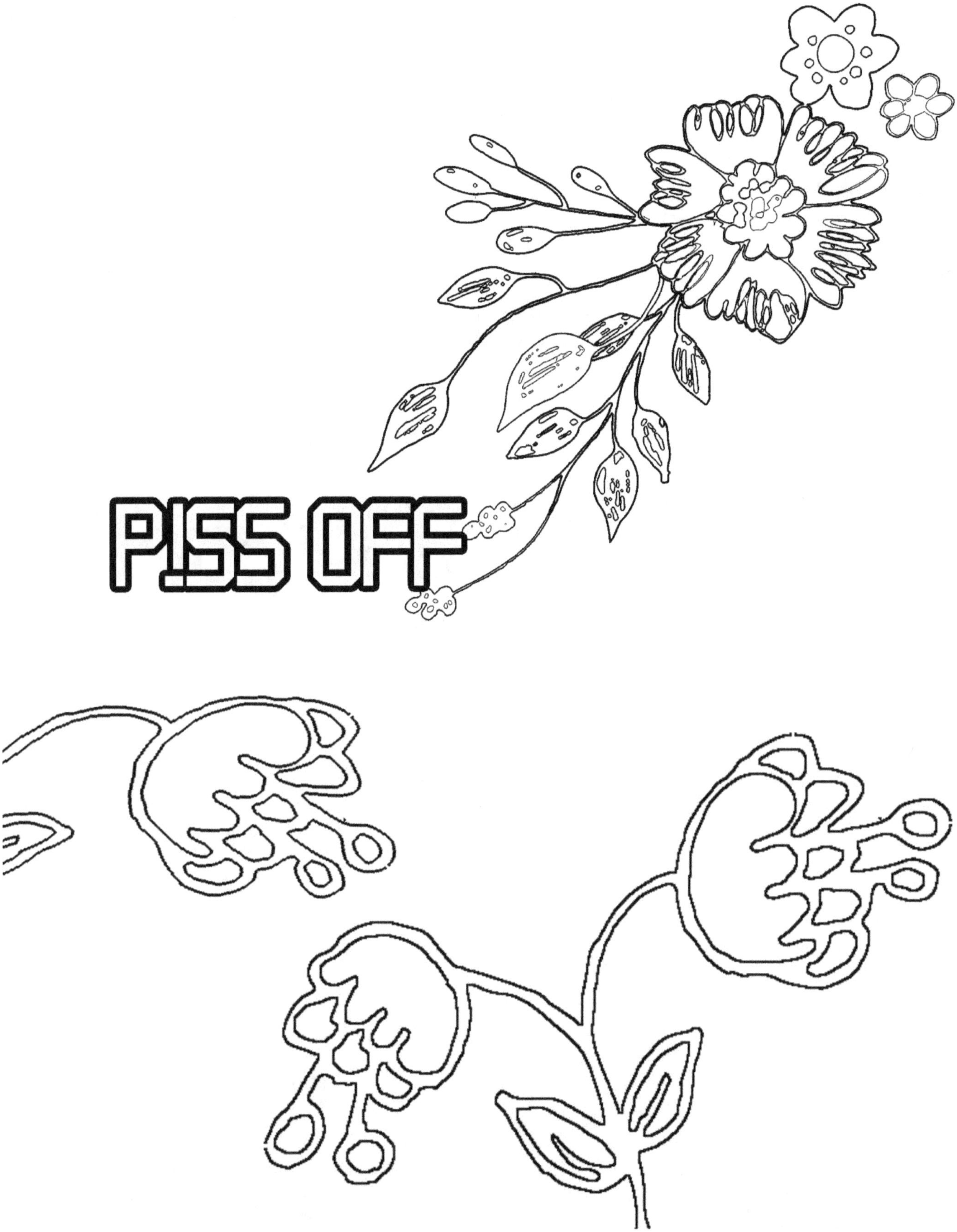
PISS OFF

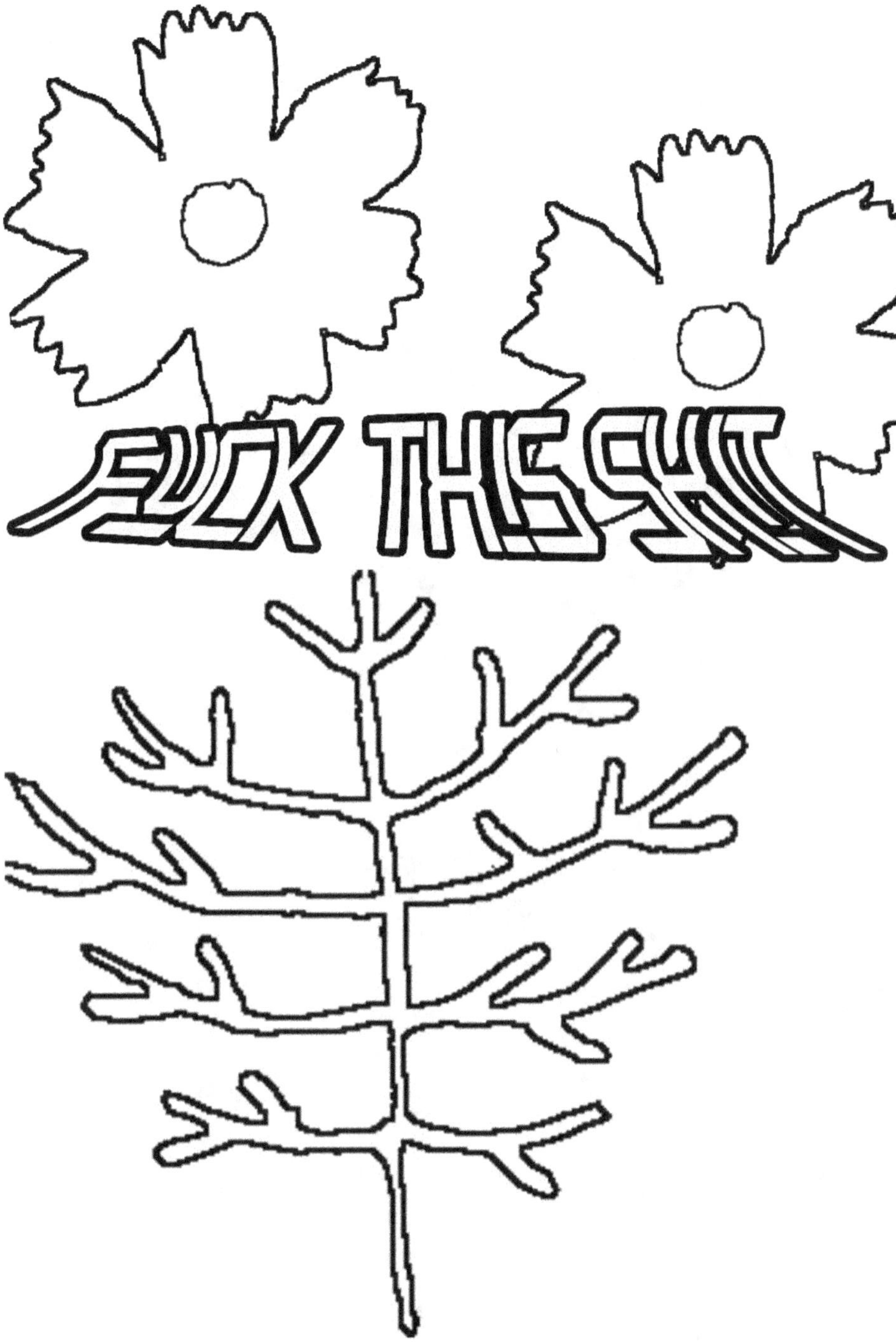
FUCK THIS SHIT

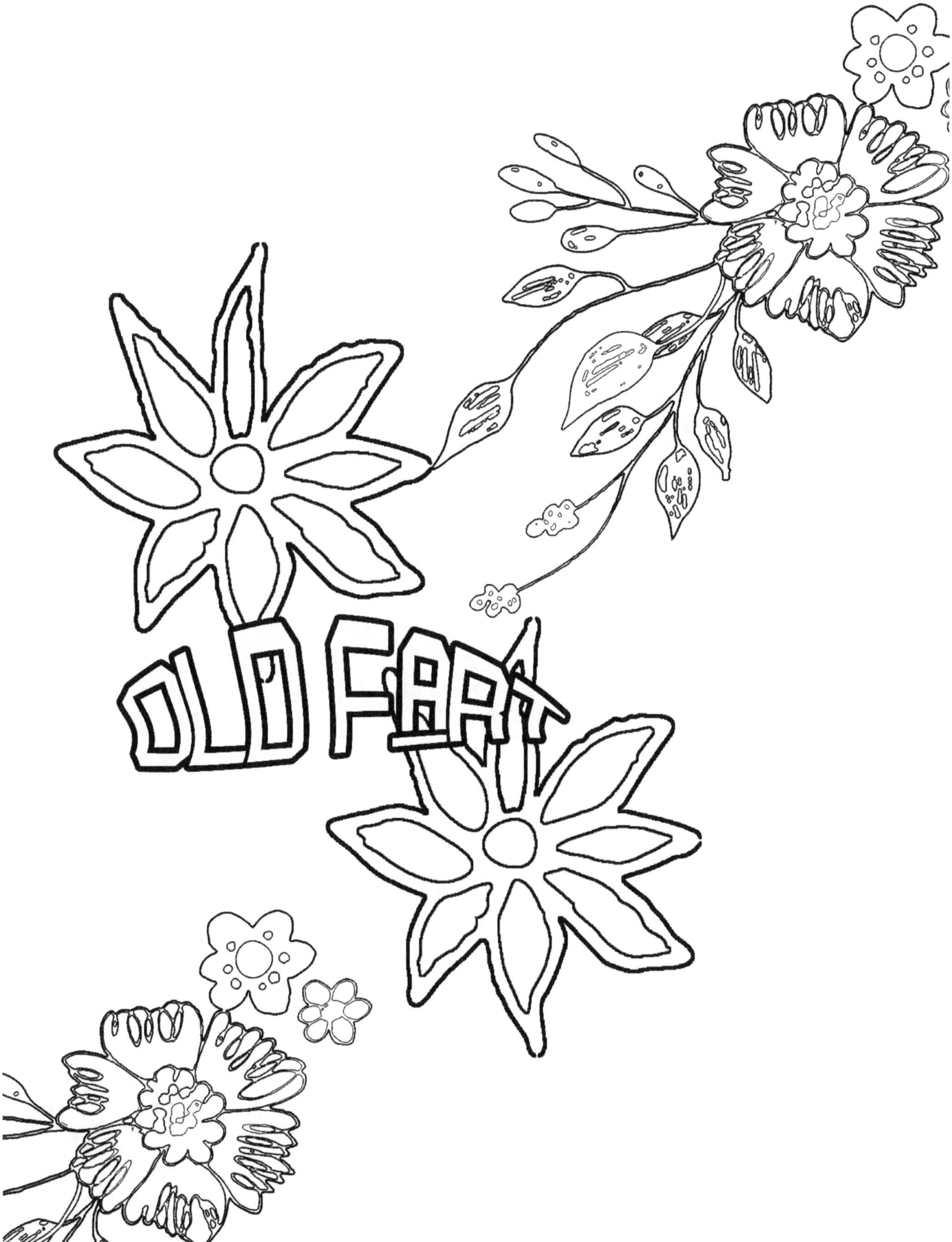
OLD FART

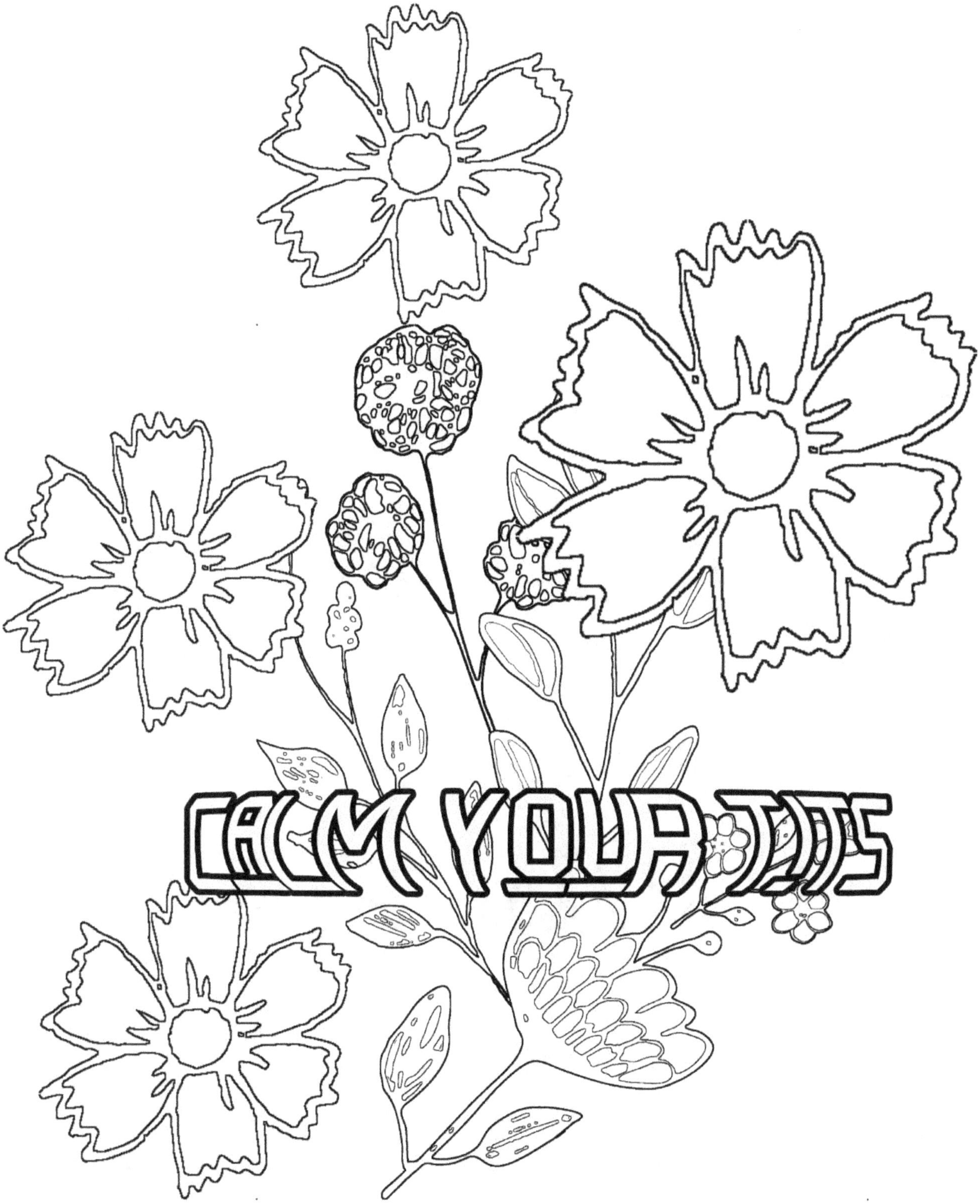
CALM YOUR TITS

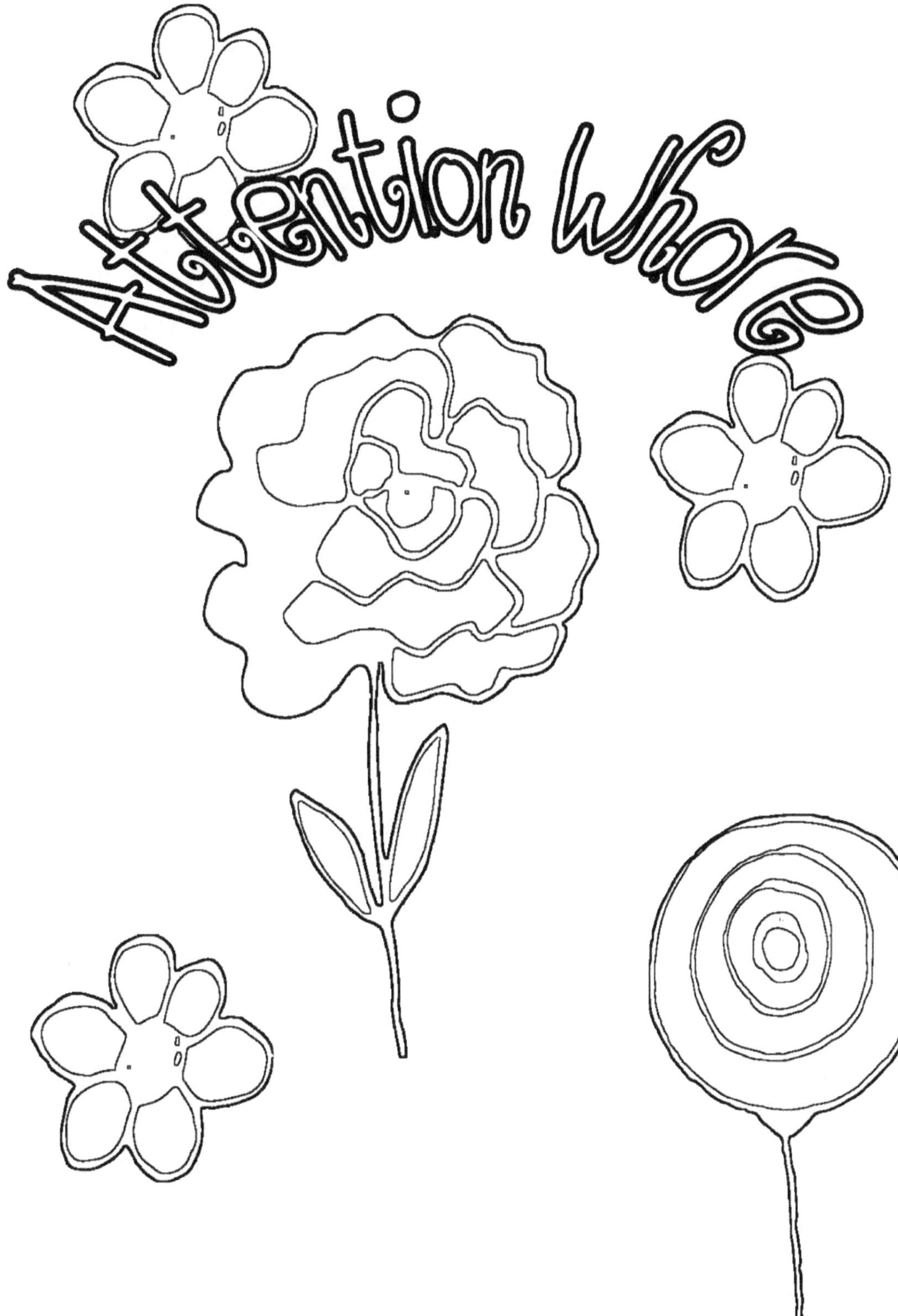
Attention Whore

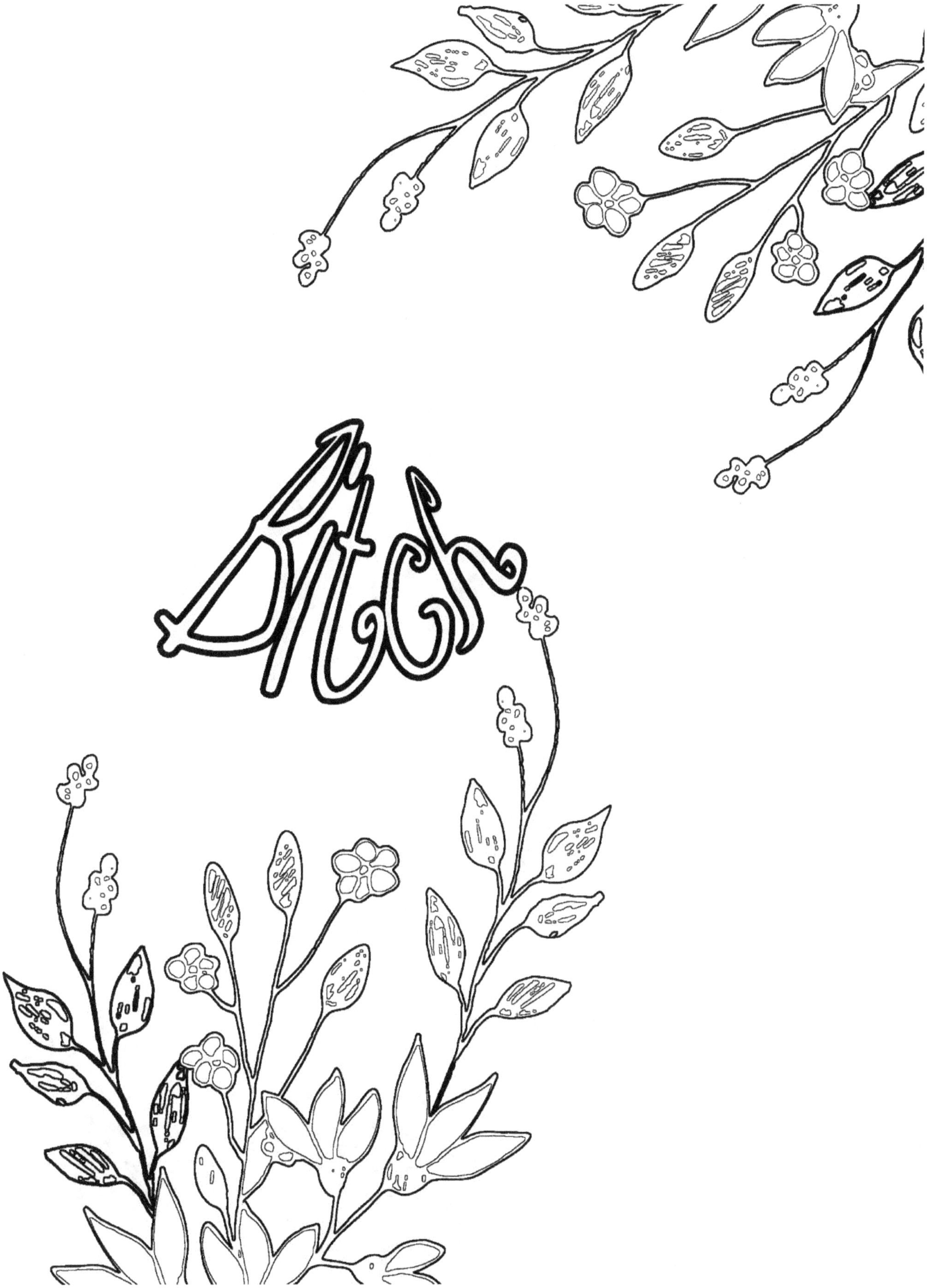
Bitch

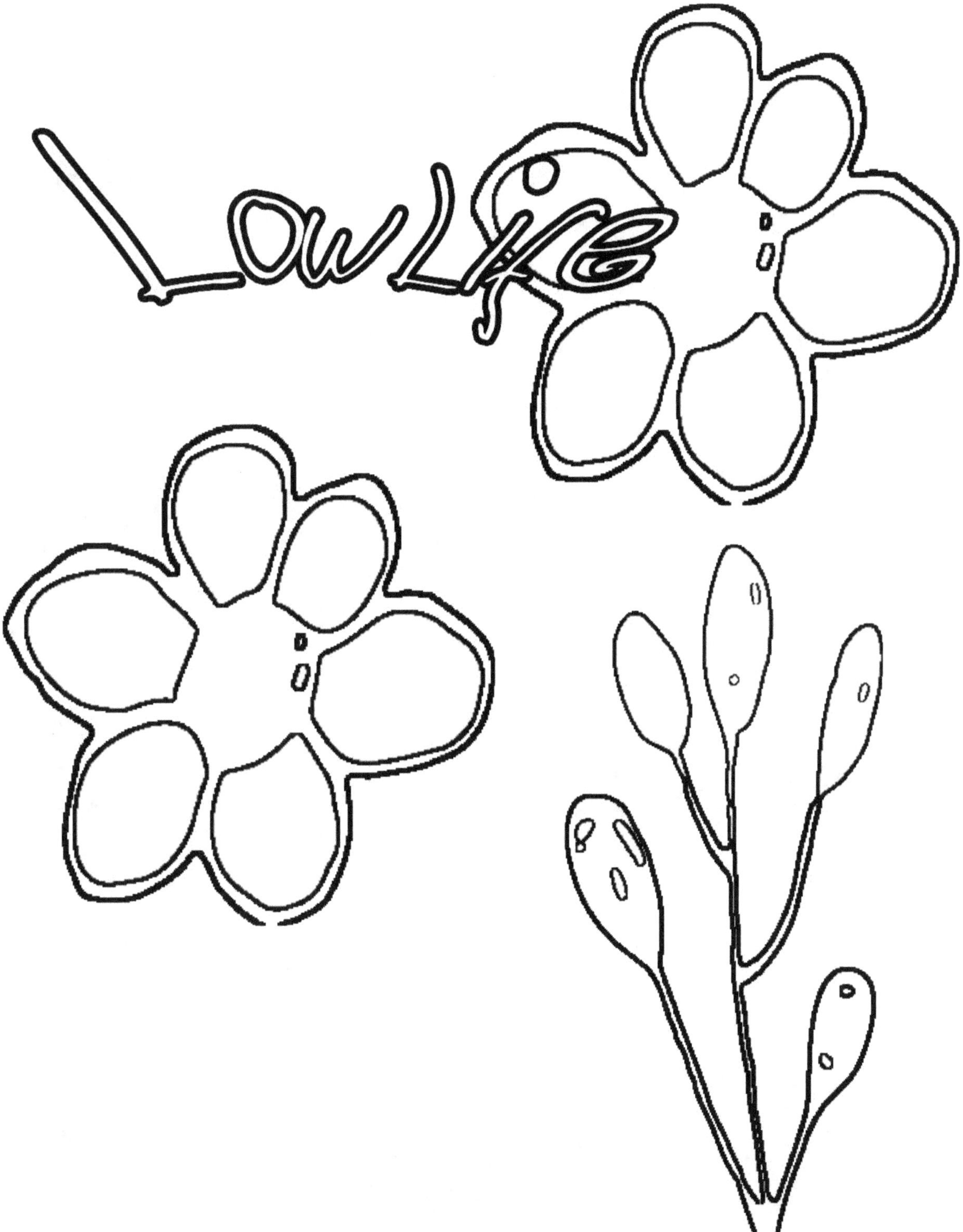
Low Life

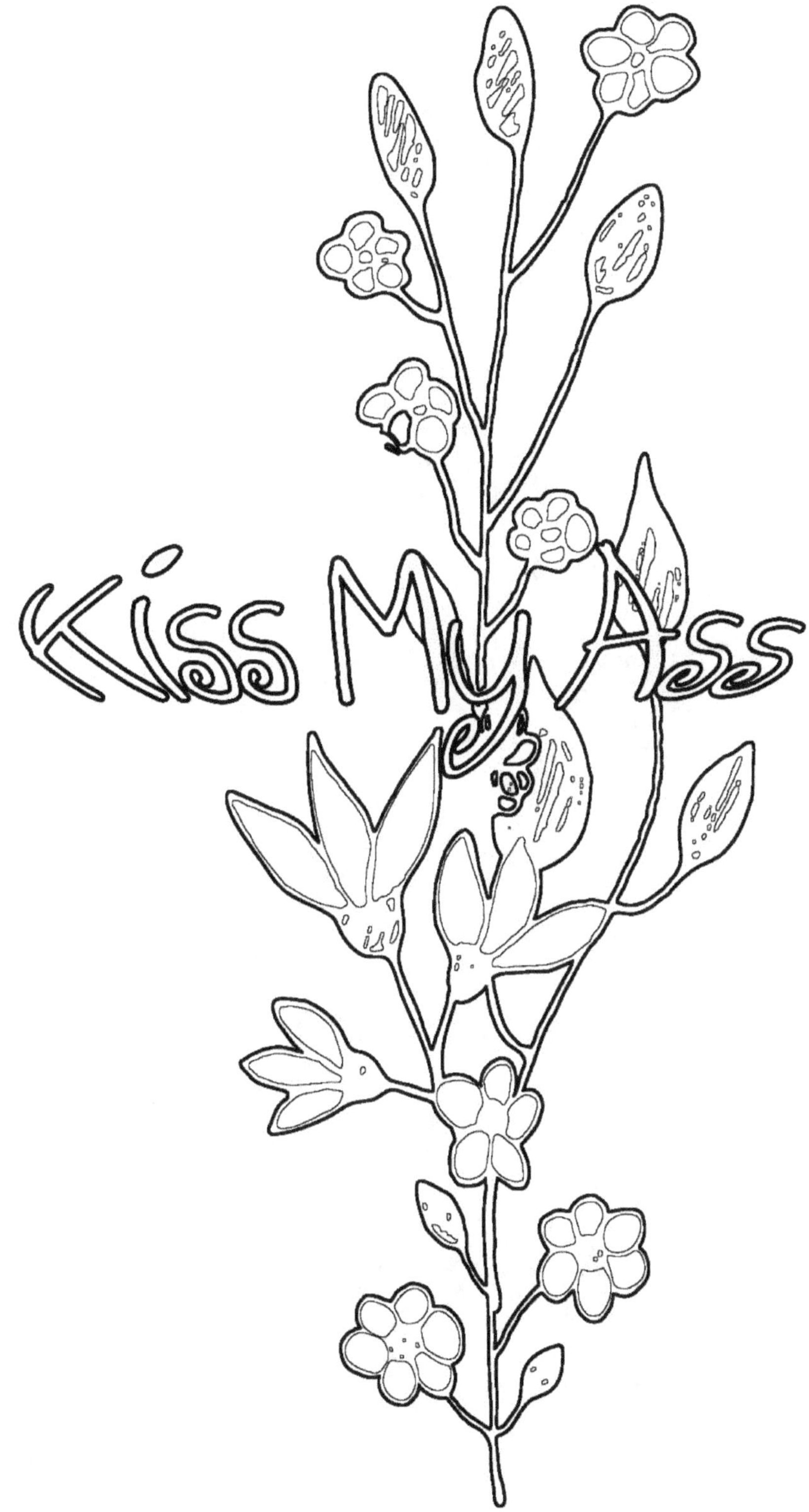
Kiss My Ass

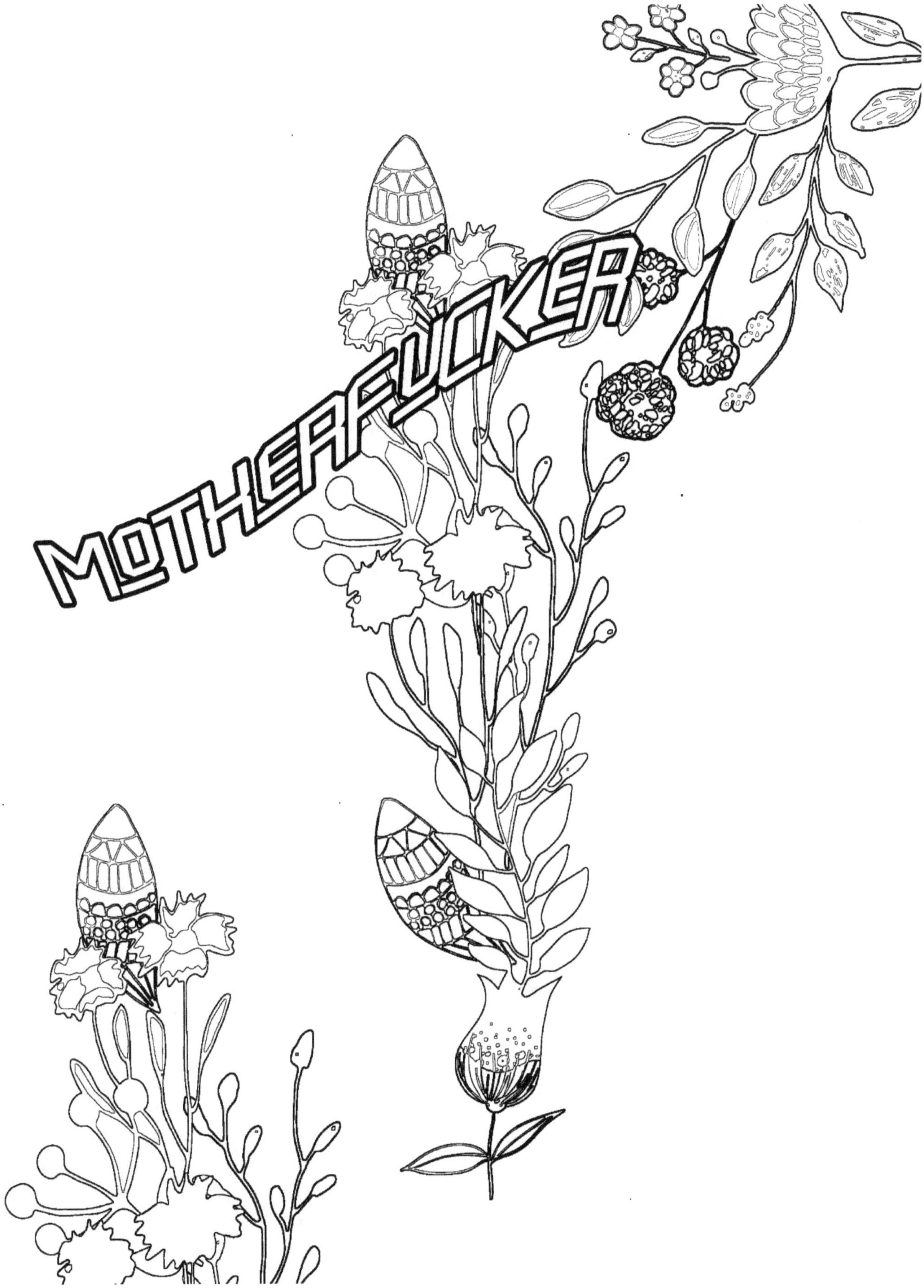
MOTHERFUCKER

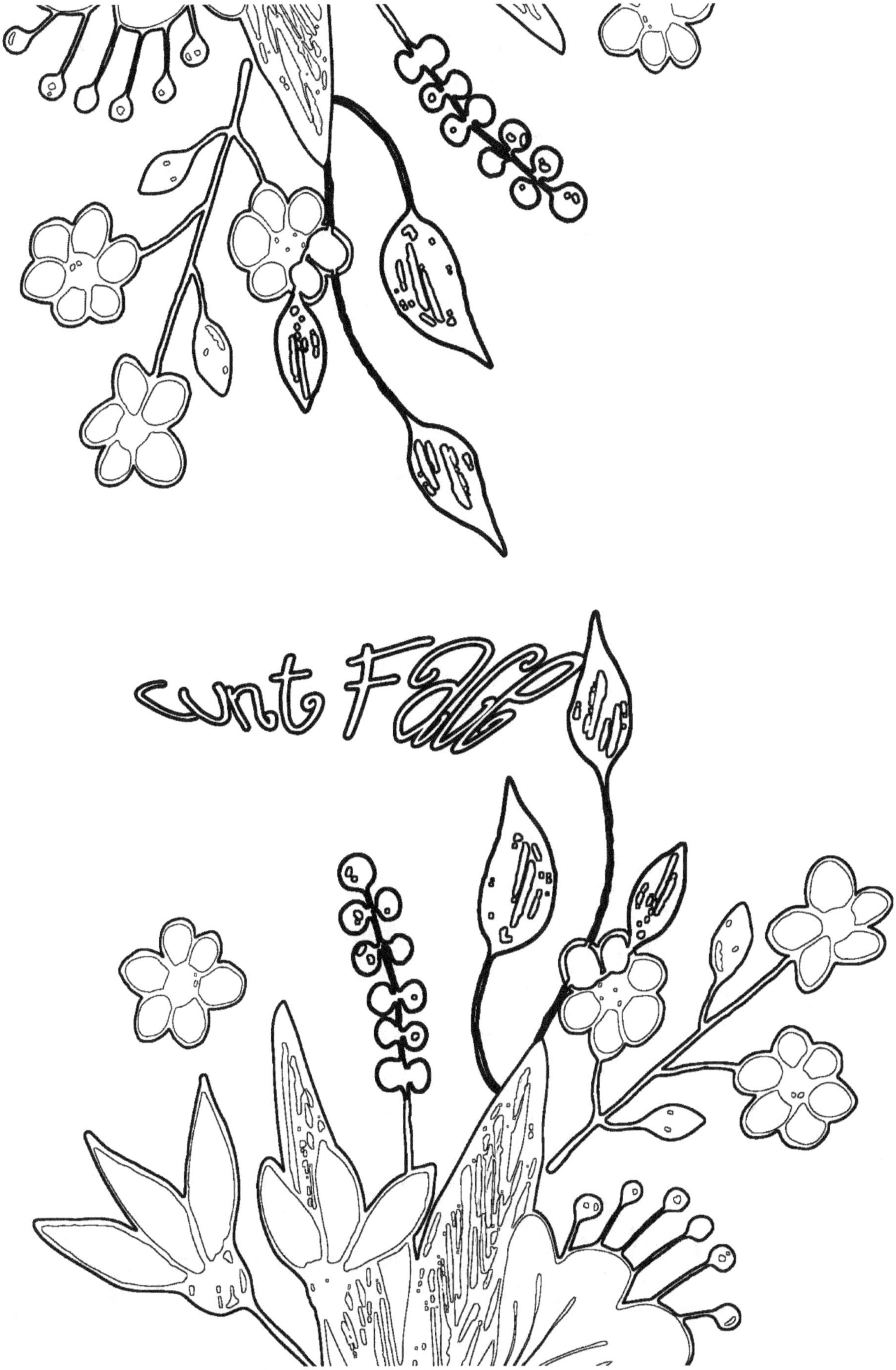
Cunt

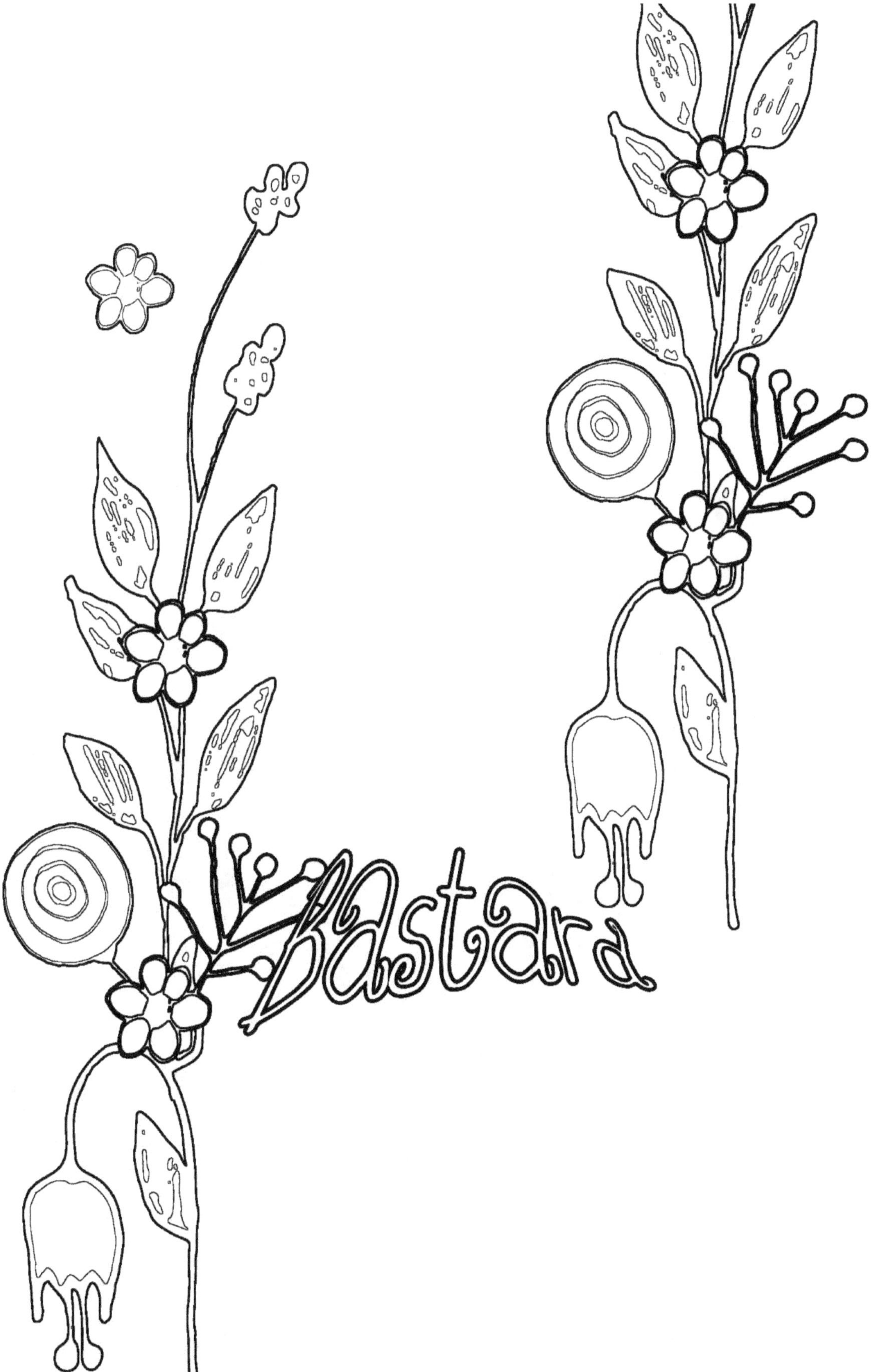
Bastara

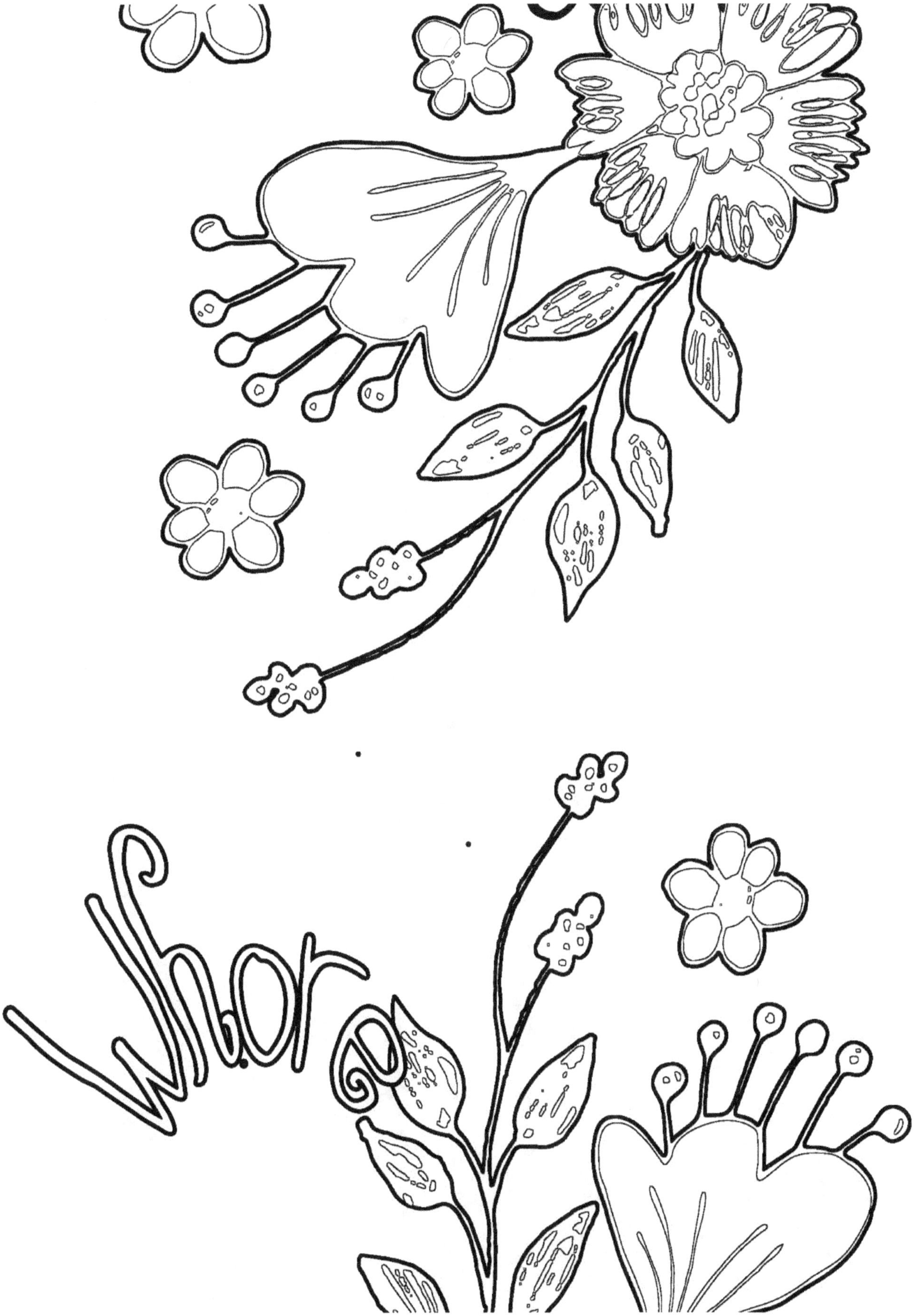
Where

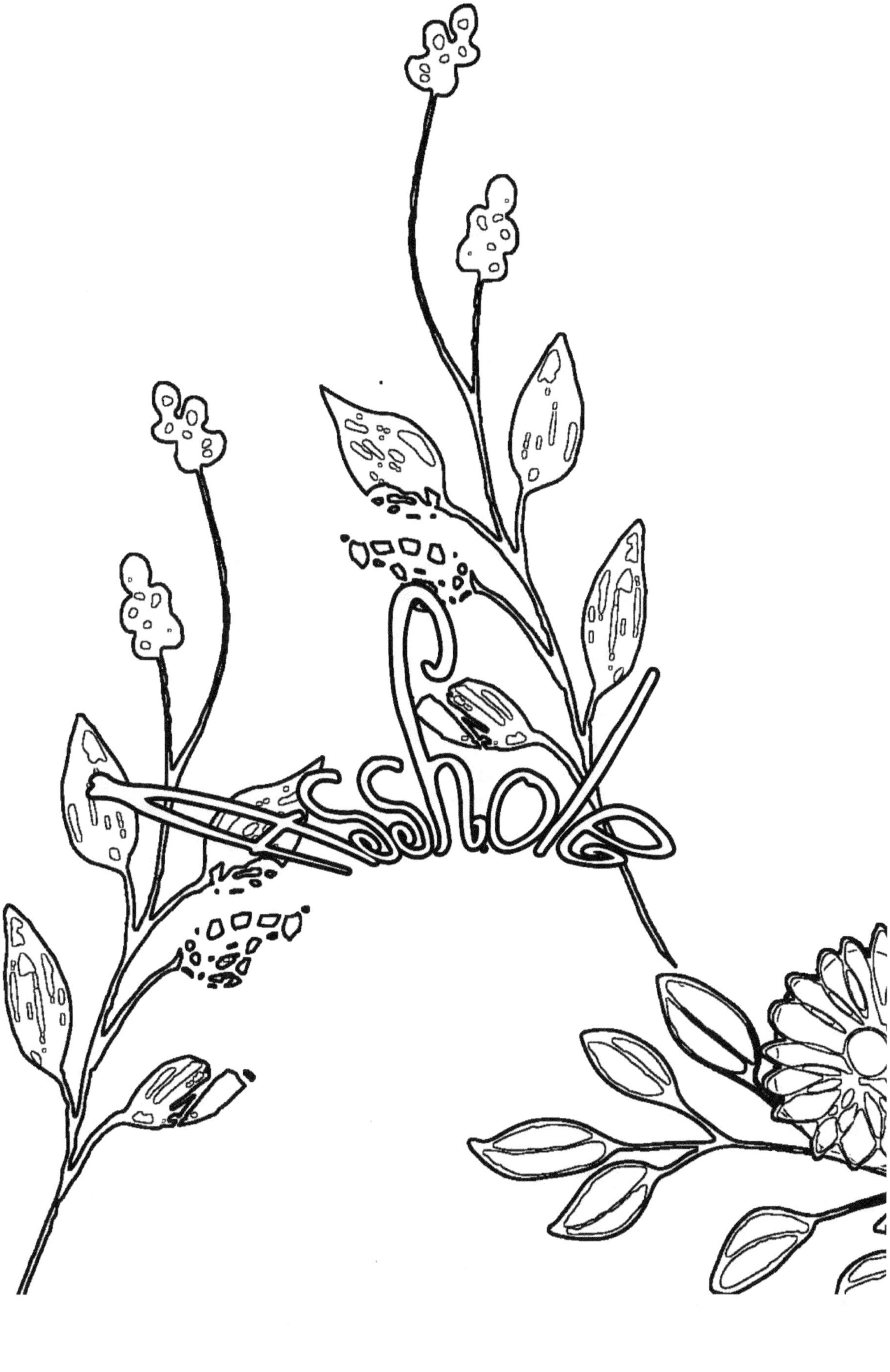
Asshole

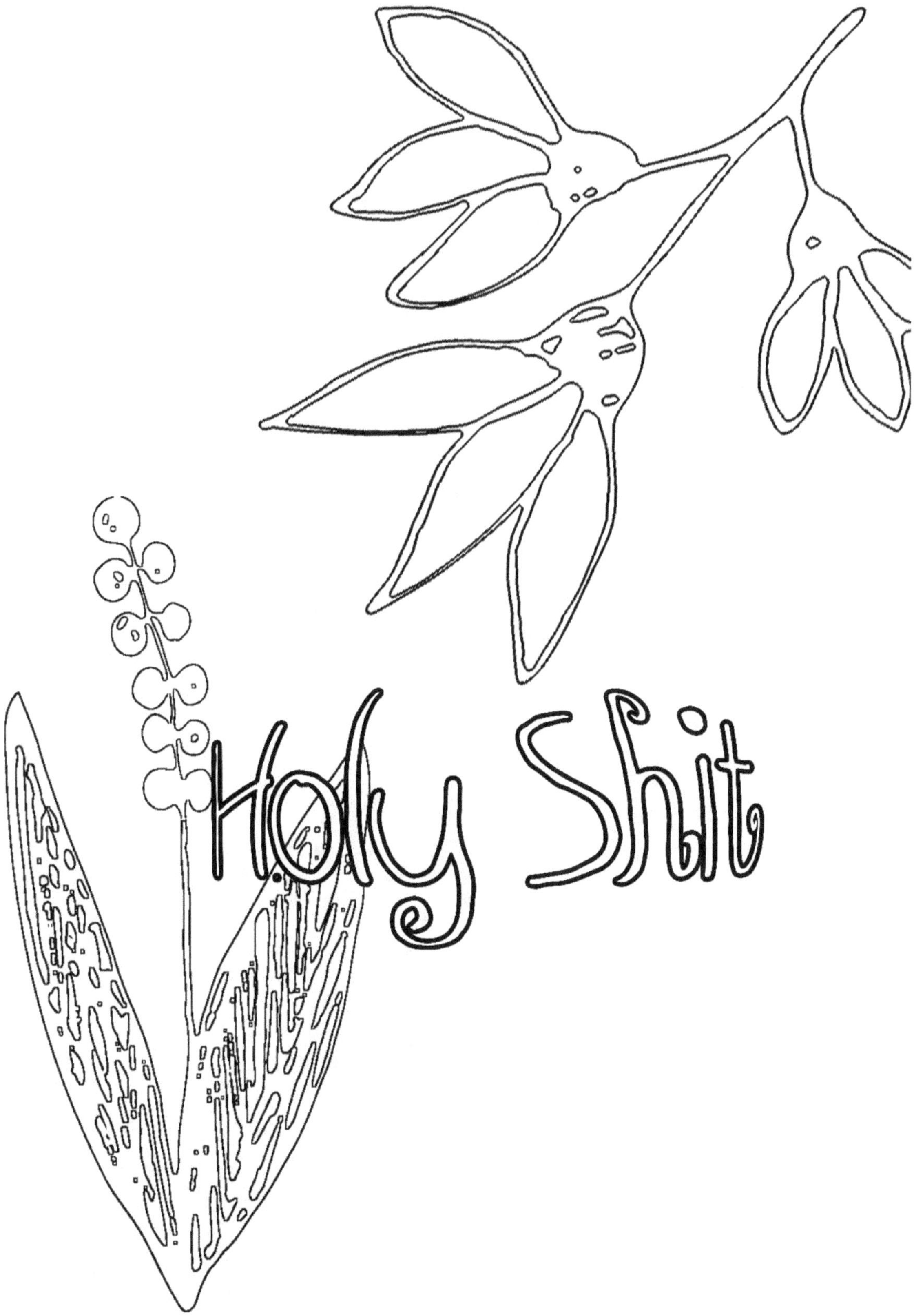
Holy Shit

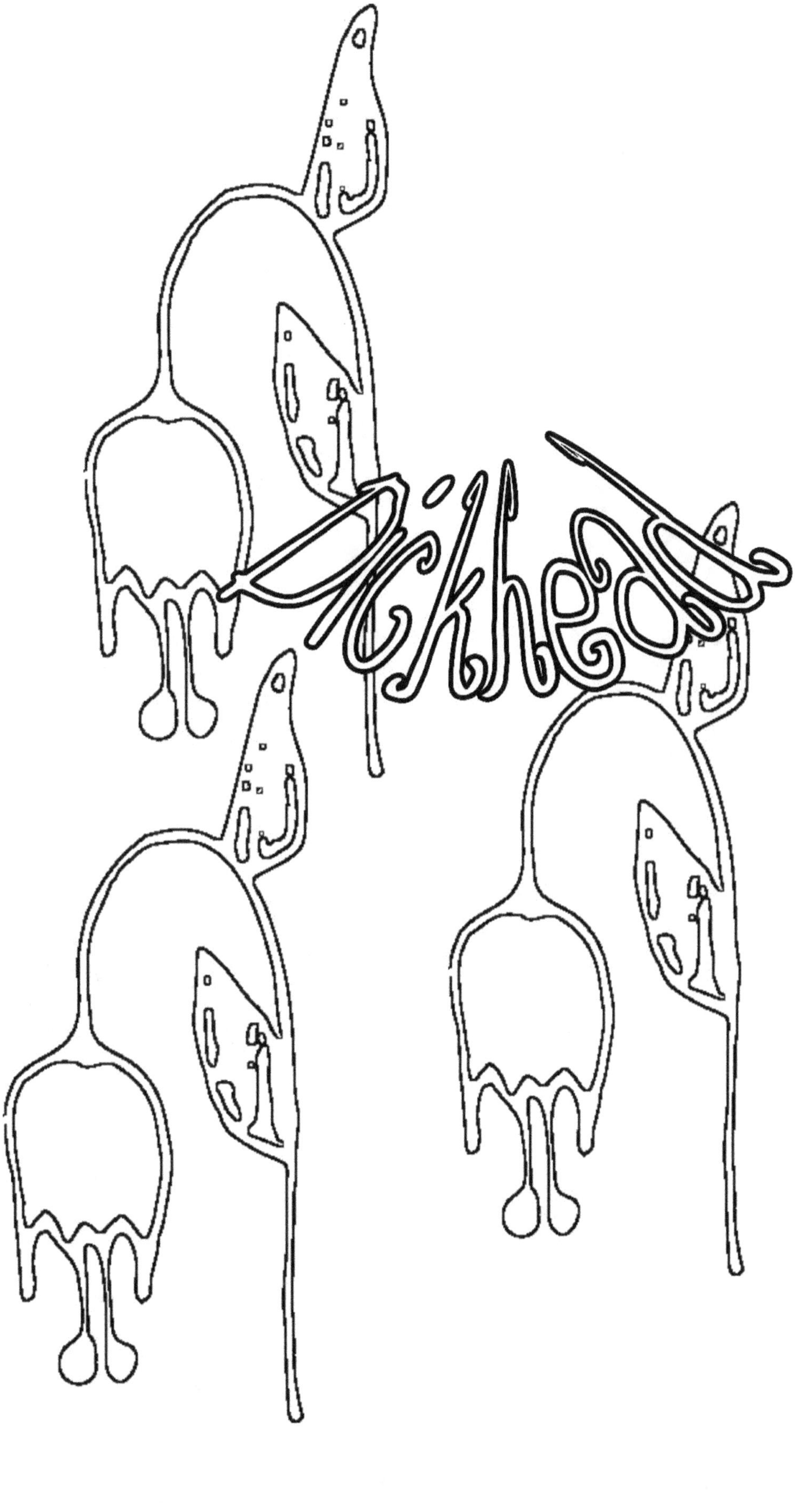
Dickhead

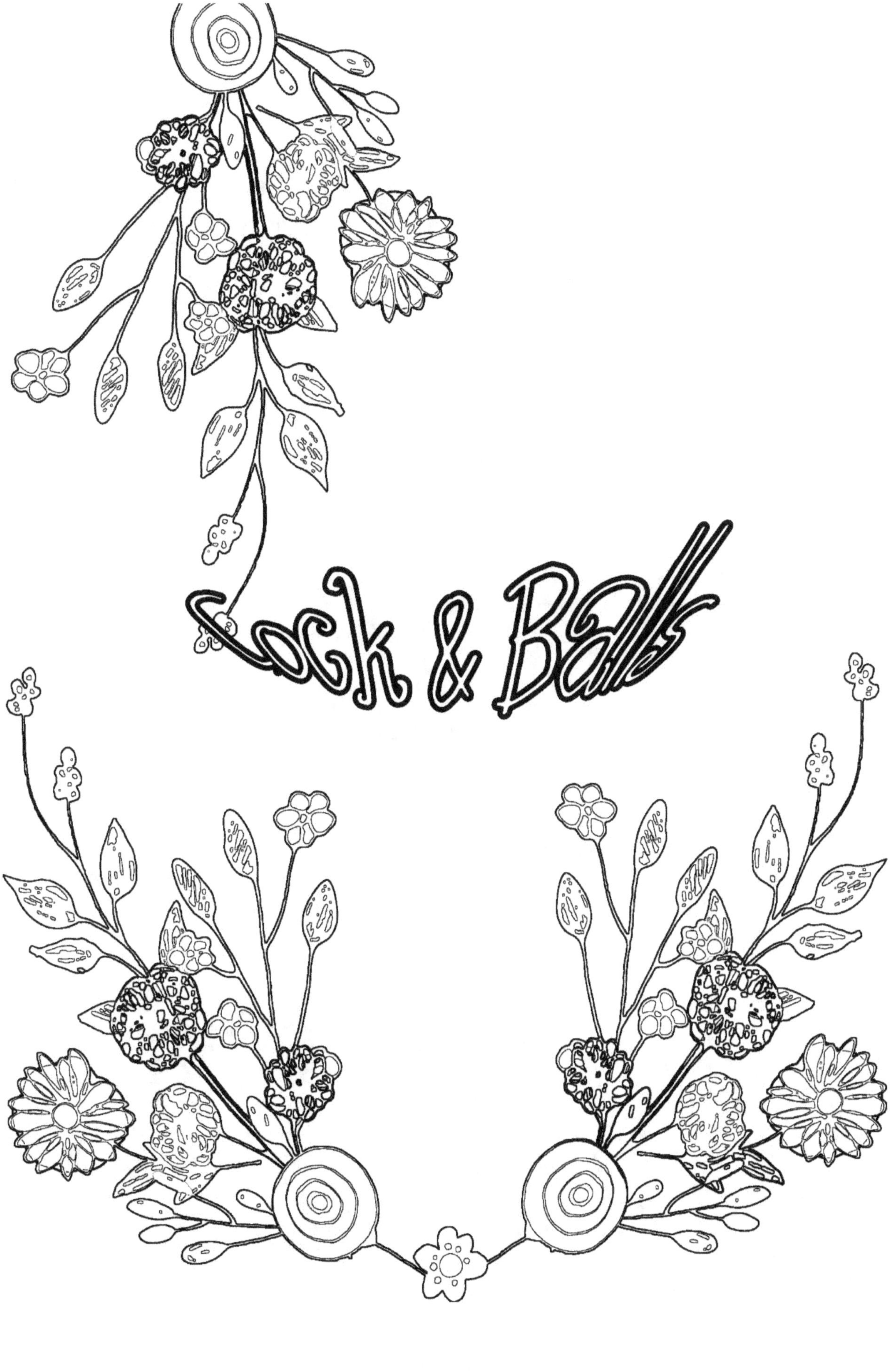
Cock & Balls

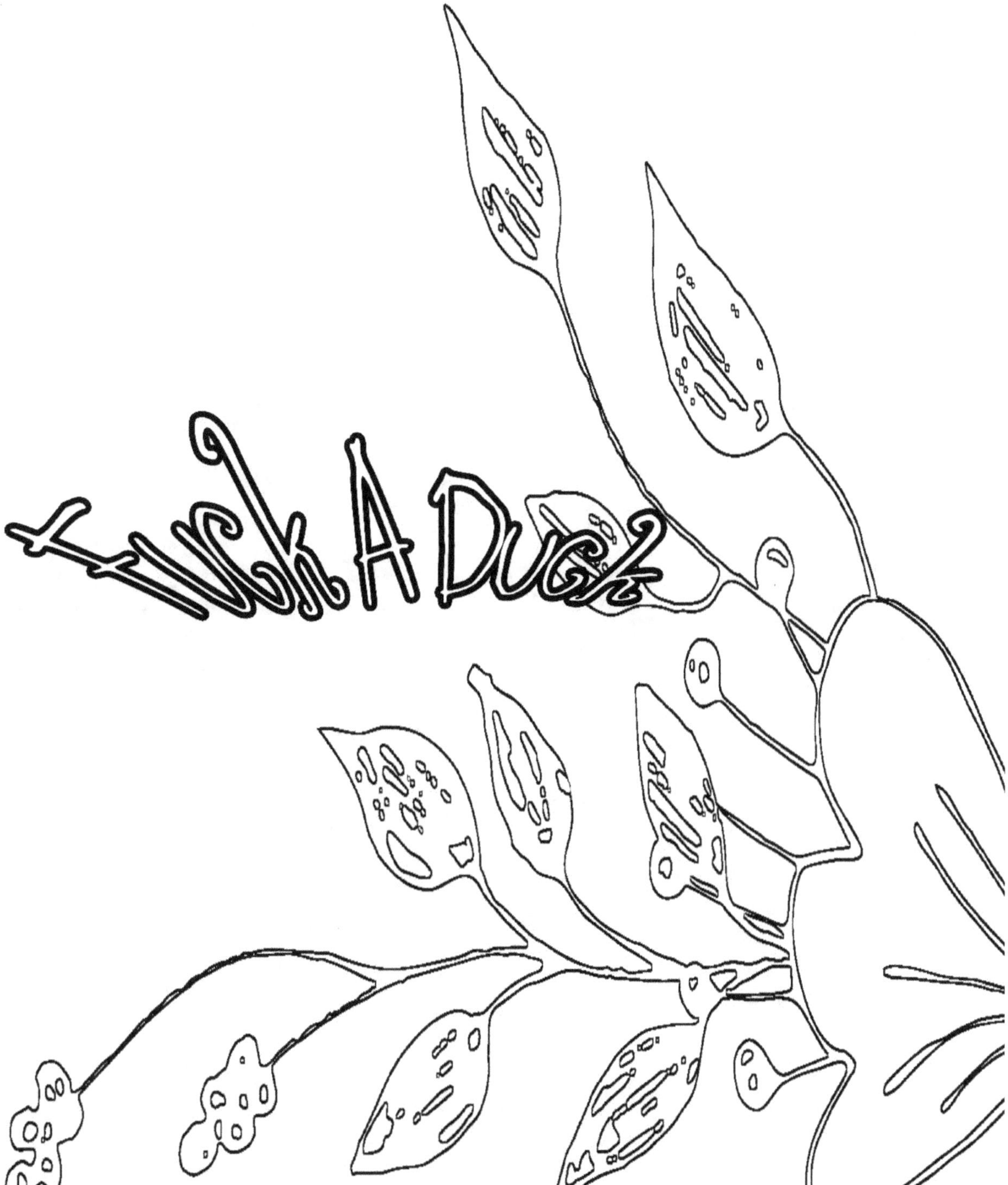
Fuck A Duck

www.ingramcontent.com/pod-product-compliance
Lightning Source LLC
Chambersburg PA
CBHW081749170526
45167CB00009B/3973
* 9 7 8 1 5 4 2 8 0 9 9 2 4 *